BRIGHTER CHILD® BOOK OF
Handwriting

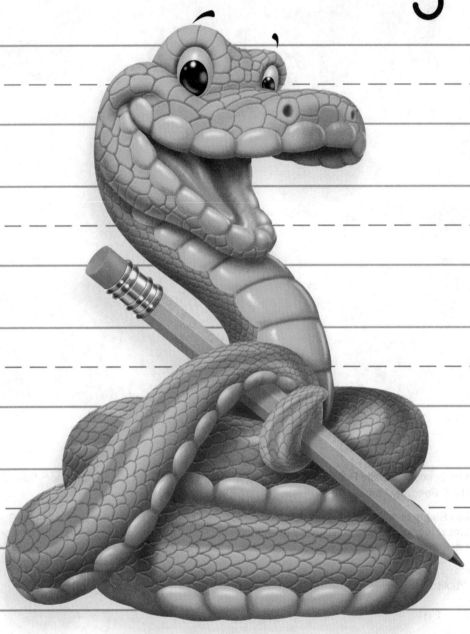

Columbus, Ohio

Send all inquiries to:
School Specialty Publishing
8720 Orion Place
Columbus, OH 43240-2111

ISBN 0-7696-8510-2

1 2 3 4 5 6 7 8 9 QPD 13 12 11 10 09

Practice by tracing the words.
Then write the words.

Name _____

alligator

apple

ant

Alaska

Bb

Practice by tracing the letter.
Then write the letter.

Name _____

B B B B B B B

b b b b b b b

Practice by tracing the words.
Then write the words.

Name _____

bear

ball

bee

Bobby

Cc

Practice by tracing the letter.
Then write the letter.

C   C   C   C   C   C   C

c   c   c   c   c   c   c

Practice by tracing the words.
Then write the words.

Name _____

cats

cookies

cards

Chuck

Dd

Practice by tracing the letter.
Then write the letter.

Name _____

D D D D D D D D

d d d d d d d d

Practice by tracing the words.
Then write the words.

Name _____

duck

dog

dance

Danny

Ee

Practice by tracing the letter.
Then write the letter.

Name _____

Practice by tracing the words.
Then write the words.

Name _____

elephant

egg

elbow

Ellie

Ff

Practice by tracing the letter.
Then write the letter.

Name _____

Practice by tracing the words.
Then write the words.

Name _____

frog

fish

fox

Florida

Gg

Practice by tracing the letter.
Then write the letter.

Name _____

G G G G G G G

g g g g g g g

Gg

Practice by tracing the words.
Then write the words.

Name _____

giraffe

grass

glasses

Gretchen

Hh

Practice by tracing the letter.
Then write the letter.

Name _____

Practice by tracing the words.
Then write the words.

Name _____

Ii

Practice by tracing the letter.
Then write the letter.

Name _____

Practice by tracing the words.
Then write the words.

Name _____

inchworm

iguana

igloo

Indiana

Jj

Practice by tracing the letter.
Then write the letter.

Name _____

J J J J J J J

j j j j j j j

Practice by tracing the words.
Then write the words.

Name _____

jaguar

jump

jam

June

Kk

Practice by tracing the letter.
Then write the letter.

Name _____

K K K K K K K K

k k k k k k k k

Practice by tracing the words.
Then write the words.

Name _____

kangaroo

kite

key

Kelsey

Ll

Practice by tracing the letter.
Then write the letter.

Name _____

Practice by tracing the words.
Then write the words.

Name _____

lion

lollipop

lick

Lori

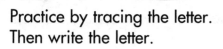
Mm

Practice by tracing the letter.
Then write the letter.

Name _____

M M M M M M M M

m m m m m m m

Practice by tracing the words.
Then write the words.

Name _____

monkey

mushroom

moon

Megan

Nn

Practice by tracing the letter.
Then write the letter.

Name _____

N N N N N N N

n n n n n n n

Practice by tracing the words.
Then write the words.

Name _____

newt

nest

note

Nebraska

Oo

Practice by tracing the letter.
Then write the letter.

Name _____

Practice by tracing the words.
Then write the words.

Name _____

ostrich

octopus

olive

Olivia

Pp

Practice by tracing the letter.
Then write the letter.

Name _____

P   P   P   P   P   P   P   P

P   P   P   P   P   P   P   P

Practice by tracing the words.
Then write the words.

Name _____

penguin

pizza

pencil

puppy

Qq

Practice by tracing the letter.
Then write the letter.

Name _____

Q   Q   Q   Q   Q   Q   Q

q   q   q   q   q   q   q

Practice by tracing the words.
Then write the words.

Name _____

quail

queen

quarter

quit

Rr

Practice by tracing the letter.
Then write the letter.

Name _____

R R R R R R R R

r r r r r r r r

Practice by tracing the words.
Then write the words.

Name _____

rabbit

ribbon

race

runs

0-7696-8510-2

Ss

Practice by tracing the letter.
Then write the letter.

Name _____

S   S   S   S   S   S   S

S   S   S   S   S   S   S

Practice by tracing the words.
Then write the words.

Name _____

seal

sun

shell

seven

Tt

Practice by tracing the letter.
Then write the letter.

Name _____

Practice by tracing the words.
Then write the words.

Name _____

turtle

tiger

tie

teach

Uu

Practice by tracing the letter.
Then write the letter.

Name _____

U U U U U U U

U U U U U U U

Uu

Practice by tracing the words.
Then write the words.

Name _____

umpire

umbrella

under

unhappy

Brighter Child® Book of Handwriting   45   0-7696-8510-2

Vv

Practice by tracing the letter.
Then write the letter.

V V V V V V V V V

V V V V V V V V

Practice by tracing the words.
Then write the words.

Name _____

vulture

violin

vest

van

Ww

Practice by tracing the letter.
Then write the letter.

W W W W W W W

w w w w w w w

Ww

Practice by tracing the words.
Then write the words.

Name _____

whale

walrus

water

wishes

Xx

Practice by tracing the letter.
Then write the letter.

Name _____

X X X X X X X X

X X X X X X X X

Practice by tracing the words.
Then write the words.

Name _____

X-ray

Xylophone

Max

Extra

Yy

Practice by tracing the letter.
Then write the letter.

Practice by tracing the words.
Then write the words.

Name _____

yak

yo-yo

yarn

Your

Zz

Practice by tracing the letter.
Then write the letter.

Name _____

Practice by tracing the words.
Then write the words.

Name _____

zebra

zipper

zoo

zigzag

Practice by tracing the words and numbers. Then write the words and numbers.

Name _____

one 1

two 2

three 3

four 4

five 5

Practice by tracing the words and numbers. Then write the words and numbers.

Name _____

six 6

seven 7

eight 8

nine 9

ten 10

Practice by tracing the words.
Then write the words.

Name _____

square

circle

rectangle

oval

Practice by tracing the words and abbreviations. Then write the words and abbreviations.

Name _____

Sunday

Sun.

Monday

Mon.

Practice by tracing the words and abbreviations. Then write the words and abbreviations.

Name _____

Tuesday

Tues.

Wednesday

Wed.

Practice by tracing the words and abbreviations. Then write the words and abbreviations.

Name _____

Thursday

Thurs.

Friday

Fri.

Days of the Week
and Abbreviations

Practice by tracing the words and abbreviations. Then write the words and abbreviations.

Name _____

Saturday

Sat.

Today

Practice by tracing the words and abbreviations. Then write the words and abbreviations.

Name _____

January

Jan.

February

Feb.

Months of the Year
and Abbreviations

Practice by tracing the words and abbreviations. Then write the words and abbreviations.

Name _____

March

Mar.

April

Apr.

Practice by tracing the words and abbreviations. Then write the words and abbreviations.

Name _____

May

June

July

August

Aug.

Months of the Year
and Abbreviations

Practice by tracing the words and abbreviations. Then write the words and abbreviations.

Name _____

September

Sept.

October

Oct.

Practice by tracing the words and abbreviations. Then write the words and abbreviations.

Name _____

November

Nov.

December

Dec.

Practice by tracing the words.
Then write the words.

Name _____

winter

spring

summer

fall

Practice by tracing the words.
Then write the words.

Name _____

pencil

book

folder

paper

Practice by tracing the words.
Then write the words.

Name _____

Mother

Father

Mom

Practice by tracing the words.
Then write the words.

Name _____

Dad

Grandma

Grandpa

Practice by tracing the words.
Then write the words.

Name _____

aunt

uncle

brother

sister

Practice by tracing the words.
Then write the words.

Name _____

apartment

library

office

park

Complete these sentences:

Name _____

I live in a _____.

My address is

Write a sentence about your neighborhood:

Practice by tracing the words.
Then write the words.

Name _____

country

city

state

town

Complete these sentences:

Name _____

My country is _____

_____•

My state is _____

_____•

My town is _____

_____•

Practice by tracing the words.
Then write the words.

Name _____

soccer

football

baseball

golf

Practice by tracing the words.
Then write the words.

Name _____

dollar $

cents ¢

penny 1¢

Practice by tracing the words.
Then write the words.

Name _____

nickel 5¢

dime 10¢

quarter 25¢

Write the correct adjective next to the picture.

Name _____

big

bigger

biggest

Write the correct adjective
next to the picture.

Name _____

good

better

best

_____

_____

_____

Practice by tracing the words.
Then write the words.

Name _____

Dear

Thank you

Sincerely

Your friend

Practice writing a thank-you note.

Name _____

Aa

Practice by tracing the letter.
Then write the letter.

Name _____

a *a* *a* *a* *a*

a

a *a* *a* *a* *a*

Practice by tracing the words.
Then write the words.

Name _____

an

and

animals

April

Bb

Practice by tracing the letter.
Then write the letter.

$\mathcal{B}$ $\mathcal{B}$ $\mathcal{B}$ $\mathcal{B}$ $\mathcal{B}$

ℓ ℓ ℓ ℓ ℓ

Practice by tracing the words.
Then write the words.

Name _____

big

boy

babble

baboon

Cc

Practice by tracing the letter.
Then write the letter.

Name _____

$\mathcal{C}$ $\mathcal{C}$ $\mathcal{C}$ $\mathcal{C}$ $\mathcal{C}$

$\mathcal{C}$ $\mathcal{C}$ $\mathcal{C}$ $\mathcal{C}$ $\mathcal{C}$

Cc

Practice by tracing the words.
Then write the words.

Name _____

can

candy

cool

count

Dd

Practice by tracing the letter.
Then write the letter.

Name _____

$\mathscr{D}$ $\mathscr{D}$ $\mathscr{D}$ $\mathscr{D}$ $\mathscr{D}$

d d d d d

Practice by tracing the words.
Then write the words.

Name _____

do

dog

dandelions

donuts

DELIVERY

Ee

Practice by tracing the letter.
Then write the letter.

Name _____

$\mathcal{E}$ $\mathcal{E}$ $\mathcal{E}$ $\mathcal{E}$ $\mathcal{E}$

$\mathscr{l}$ $\mathscr{l}$ $\mathscr{l}$ $\mathscr{l}$ $\mathscr{l}$

**Practice by tracing the words.
Then write the words.**

Name _____

each

eat

eels

eighty

Brighter Child® Book of Handwriting

93

0-7696-8510-2

Ff

Practice by tracing the letter.
Then write the letter.

Name _____

$\mathcal{F}$ $\mathcal{F}$ $\mathcal{F}$ $\mathcal{F}$ $\mathcal{F}$

f f f f f

Practice by tracing the words.
Then write the words.

Name _____

far

fat

fluff

feast

Gg

Practice by tracing the letter.
Then write the letter.

Name _____

Practice by tracing the words.
Then write the words.

Name _____

gag

gift

good

giggle

0-7696-8510-2

Practice by tracing the letter.
Then write the letter.

Name _____

Practice by tracing the words.
Then write the words.

Name _____

his

happy

he

hello

Ii

Practice by tracing the letter.
Then write the letter.

Name _____

**Practice by tracing the words.
Then write the words.**

if

in

idea

itch

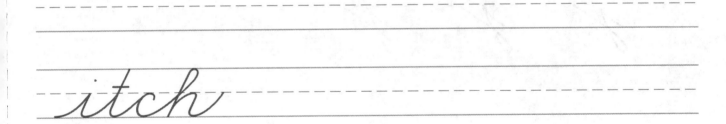

Jj

Practice by tracing the letter.
Then write the letter.

Name _____

Practice by tracing the words.
Then write the words.

Name _____

jam

job

jazz

junk

Kk

Practice by tracing the letter.
Then write the letter.

Name _____

$\mathcal{K}$ $\mathcal{K}$ $\mathcal{K}$ $\mathcal{K}$ $\mathcal{K}$ $\mathcal{K}$

k k k k k k

Practice by tracing the words.
Then write the words.

Name _____

kid

key

Kick

keep

Practice by tracing the letter.
Then write the letter.

Name _____

$\mathscr{L}$ $\mathscr{L}$ $\mathscr{L}$ $\mathscr{L}$ $\mathscr{L}$ $\mathscr{L}$ $\mathscr{L}$

$\mathscr{l}$ $\mathscr{l}$ $\mathscr{l}$ $\mathscr{l}$ $\mathscr{l}$ $\mathscr{l}$

Practice by tracing the words.
Then write the words.

Name _____

low

land

lamb

little

Mm

Practice by tracing the letter.
Then write the letter.

Name _____

m m m m m

mm m m m m

Practice by tracing the words.
Then write the words.

Name _____

mad

milk

monkeys

merry

Nn

Practice by tracing the letter.
Then write the letter.

Name _____

n n n n n

m m m m m

Practice by tracing the words.
Then write the words.

Name _____

nap

name

near

night

Oo

Practice by tracing the letter.
Then write the letter.

Name _____

O O O O O

O O O O O

Practice by tracing the words.
Then write the words.

Name _____

out

often

once

order

Brighter Child® Book of Handwriting

113

0-7696-8510-2

Pp

Practice by tracing the letter.
Then write the letter.

Name _____

𝒫 𝒫 𝒫 𝒫 𝒫

𝓅 𝓅 𝓅 𝓅 𝓅

Practice by tracing the words.
Then write the words.

Name _____

pan

pet

pick

paper

Qq

Practice by tracing the letter.
Then write the letter.

Name _____

Q   Q   Q   Q   Q

q   q   q   q   q

Practice by tracing the words.
Then write the words.

Name _____

quit

quick

quart

quiet

Rr

Practice by tracing the letter.
Then write the letter.

Name _____

R R R R R

N N N N N

Practice by tracing the words.
Then write the words.

Name _____

rat

run

rear

road

Ss

Practice by tracing the letter.
Then write the letter.

Name _____

Practice by tracing the words.
Then write the words.

Name _____

see

sing

stand

stow

0-7696-8510-2

Tt

Practice by tracing the letter.
Then write the letter.

Name _____

Practice by tracing the words.
Then write the words.

Name _____

the

tip

told

twist

Uu

Practice by tracing the letter.
Then write the letter.

Name _____

Practice by tracing the words.
Then write the words.

Name _____

use

under

until

unhappy

Vv

Practice by tracing the letter.
Then write the letter.

Name _____

$\mathcal{V}$ $\mathcal{V}$ $\mathcal{V}$ $\mathcal{V}$ $\mathcal{V}$

$\mathcal{N}$ $\mathcal{N}$ $\mathcal{N}$ $\mathcal{N}$ $\mathcal{N}$

Practice by tracing the words.
Then write the words.

Name _____

very

vote

vine

vest

Ww

Practice by tracing the letter.
Then write the letter.

$\mathscr{W}$ $\mathscr{W}$ $\mathscr{W}$ $\mathscr{W}$ $\mathscr{W}$

w w w w w

Practice by tracing the words.
Then write the words.

wet

west

wall

winter

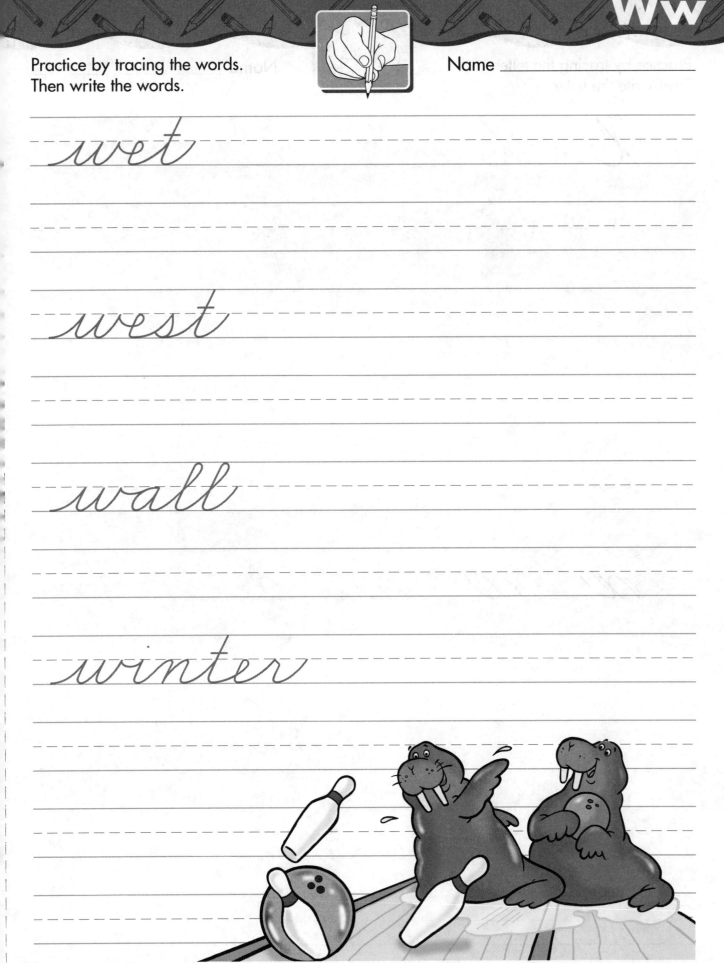

Xx

Practice by tracing the letter.
Then write the letter.

Name _____

$\mathcal{X}$ $\mathcal{X}$ $\mathcal{X}$ $\mathcal{X}$ $\mathcal{X}$

$\mathcal{N}$ $\mathcal{N}$ $\mathcal{N}$ $\mathcal{N}$ $\mathcal{N}$

Practice by tracing the words.
Then write the words.

Name _____

x-ray

box

extra

xylophone

X-RAY
MACHINE

FOX IN BOX

Yy

Practice by tracing the letter.
Then write the letter.

Name _____

Y Y Y Y Y Y

y y y y y

Practice by tracing the words.
Then write the words.

Name _____

you

yard

year

yellow

Zz

Practice by tracing the letter.
Then write the letter.

Name _____

𝒵 𝒵 𝒵 𝒵 𝒵

𝒵 𝒵 𝒵 𝒵 𝒵

Practice by tracing the words.
Then write the words.

Name _____

zero

zoom

zone

zipper

0-7696-8510-2

Numbers

Practice by tracing the words and numbers. Then write the words and numbers.

Name _____

one 1

two 2

three 3

four 4

five 5

Practice by tracing the words and numbers. Then write the words and numbers.

Name _____

six 6

seven 7

eight 8

nine 9

ten 10

Practice by tracing the words.
Then write the words.

Name _____

square

circle

rectangle

oval

Practice by tracing the words.
Then write the words.

Name _____

red

blue

yellow

orange

Days of the Week
and Abbreviations

Practice by tracing the words and abbreviations. Then write the words and abbreviations.

Name _____

Sunday

Sun.

Monday

Mon.

Practice by tracing the words and abbreviations. Then write the words and abbreviations.

Name _____

Tuesday

Tues.

Wednesday

Wed.

Days of the Week
and Abbreviations

Practice by tracing the words and abbreviations. Then write the words and abbreviations.

Name _____

Thursday

Thurs.

Friday

Fri.

Practice by tracing the words and
abbreviations. Then write the words
and abbreviations.

Name _____

Saturday

Sat.

Today

Practice by tracing the words and abbreviations. Then write the words and abbreviations.

Name _____

January

Jan.

February

Feb.

Practice by tracing the words and abbreviations. Then write the words and abbreviations.

Name _____

March

Mar.

April

Apr.

Months of the Year
and Abbreviations

Practice by tracing the words and abbreviations. Then write the words and abbreviations.

Name _____

May

June

July

August

Aug.

Practice by tracing the words and abbreviations. Then write the words and abbreviations.

Name _____

September

Sept.

October

Oct.

Months of the Year
and Abbreviations

Practice by tracing the words and abbreviations. Then write the words and abbreviations.

Name _____

November

Nov.

December

Dec.

Practice by tracing the words.
Then write the words.

Name _____

winter

spring

summer

fall

Practice by tracing the words.
Then write the words.

Name _____

math

music

art

gym

Practice by tracing the words.
Then write the words.

Name _____

pencil

book

folder

paper

151

Practice by tracing the words.
Then write the words.

Name _____

Mother

Father

Mom

Practice by tracing the words.
Then write the words.

Name _____

Dad

Grandma

Grandpa

Practice by tracing the words.
Then write the words.

Name _____

aunt

uncle

brother

sister

Write the correct adjective
next to the picture.

Name _____

long

longer

longest

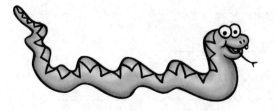

Math Words

Practice by tracing the words.
Then write the words.

Name _____

add

subtract

multiply

divide

Practice by tracing the words.
Then write the words.

Name _____

habitat

experiment

food chain

water cycle

Practice by tracing the words.
Then write the words.

Name _____

paint

draw

sketch

sculpture

Traditional Manuscript

Aa Bb Cc Dd Ee Ff Gg
Hh Ii Jj Kk Ll Mm Nn
Oo Pp Qq Rr Ss Tt Uu
Vv Ww Xx Yy Zz
0 1 2 3 4 5 6 7 8 9

anteater
bear
cat
dog
elephant
frog
goose
hippopotamus
iguana
jaguar
kangaroo
lion
monkey
numbat
owl
pig
quail
rabbit
squirrel
turtle
unicorn
vulture
walrus
x-ray
yak
zebra

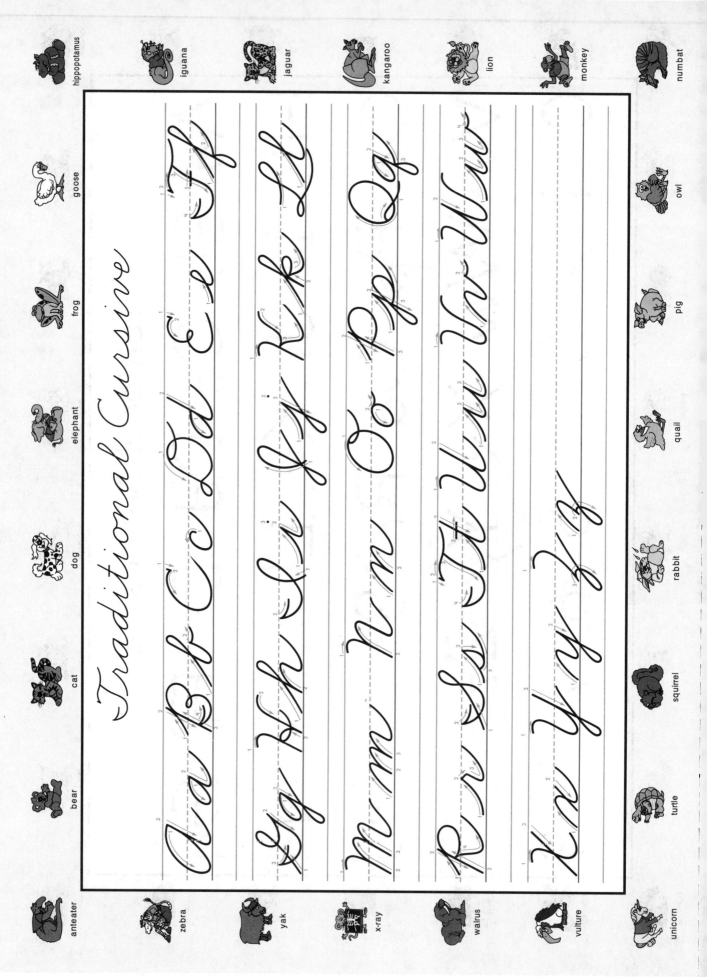

Traditional Cursive

Aa Bb Cc Dd Ee Ff
Gg Hh Ii Jj Kk Ll
Mm Nn Oo Pp Qq
Rr Ss Tt Uu Vv Ww
Xx Yy Zz

hippopotamus iguana jaguar kangaroo lion monkey numbat
goose owl
frog pig
elephant quail
dog rabbit
cat squirrel
bear turtle
anteater zebra yak x-ray walrus vulture unicorn